Lingo Dingo
and the Polish
astronaut

Written by Mark Pallis

Illustrated by James Cottell

For my awesome sons Oscar and Felix - MP

For Sophia - JC

LINGO DINGO AND THE POLISH ASTRONAUT

Story edited by Natascha Biebow, Blue Elephant Storyshaping
First Printing, 2022
ISBN: 978-1-913595-95-1
NeuWestendPress.com

Lingo Dingo
and the Polish
astronaut

Written by Mark Pallis

Illustrated by James Cottell

NEU WESTEND
— PRESS —

This is Lingo. She's a Dingo and she loves helping.
Anyone. Anytime. Anyhow.

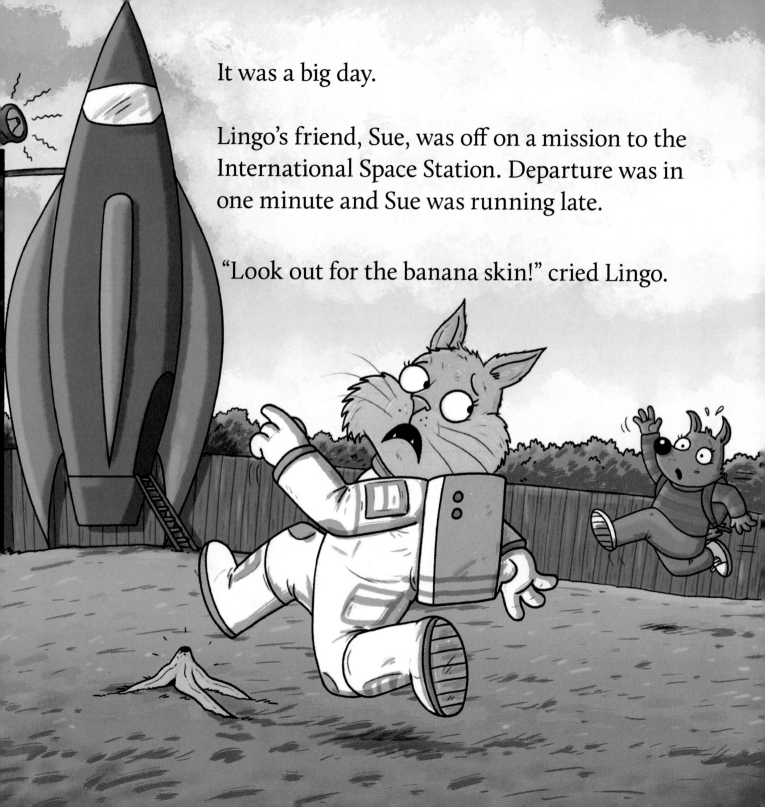

It was a big day.

Lingo's friend, Sue, was off on a mission to the International Space Station. Departure was in one minute and Sue was running late.

"Look out for the banana skin!" cried Lingo.

"I'll be OK, but the mission is over," said Sue.

"I can help!" said Lingo.

But there were only thirty seconds to launch: hurry Lingo!

Quick as a shooting star, Lingo climbed up into the rocket.

"Don't forget this. It's a battery for the Space Station," said Sue.

The countdown began: Five, four...

Lingo buckled up.

3...

She felt nervous.

2...

1...

Blast off!

Lingo soon arrived at the International Space Station.

She was in space and she could f l o a t !

"Witam!" said an astronaut. "Nazywam się Rex. Jestem astronautą."
Lingo tried a reply in Polish, "Nazywam się Lingo."

Witam = Welcome; **Nazywam się** = My name is
Jestem astronautą = I am an astronaut

"Chodź," said Rex. He led Lingo around the Space station.

"Toaleta."

"Laboratorium."

"Sypialnia. A to mój pluszowy miś."

chodź = come; toaleta = the toilet; laboratorium = the laboratory
Sypialnia = the bedroom; A to mój pluszowy miś = and my teddybear

Suddenly a BEEPING blared out!

"Masz nową baterię?" asked Rex.

Lingo wasn't sure what 'bateria' meant. She checked her pockets.

Masz nową baterię? = have you got the new battery?
bateria = battery; **nowa** = new

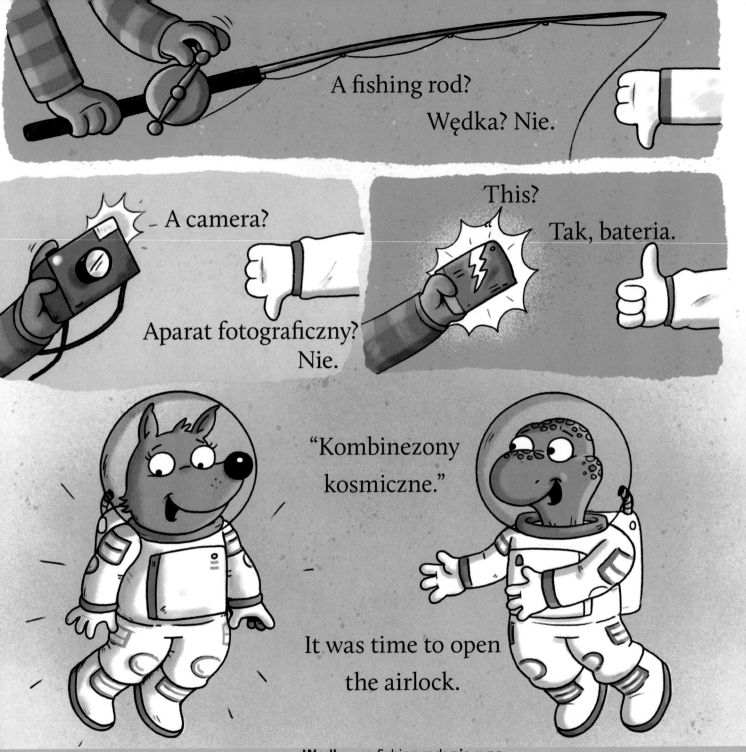

Wędka = a fishing rod; nie = no
aparat fotograficzny = a camera; tak = yes; kombinezony kosmiczne = space suits on!

"Obróć w lewo," said Rex, pointing to the handle.

Lingo turned it right. "Nie w prawo,
w lewo!" cried Rex. Lingo turned it left
and the hatch swung open.

prawo = right; **lewo** = left
nie w prawo, w lewo = not right, left; **obróć w lewo** = turn it to the left

Space was waiting for them!
They got straight to work changing the battery.
"Podaj mi śrubokręt, proszę," said Rex.

Lingo passed Rex the screwdriver and he
screwed the new battery into place.

śrubokręt = screwdriver; **proszę** = please
Podaj mi śrubokręt = pass me the screwdriver

"Udało się! Przybij piątkę," he said.

Lingo realised Rex wanted
a high five.

Success!

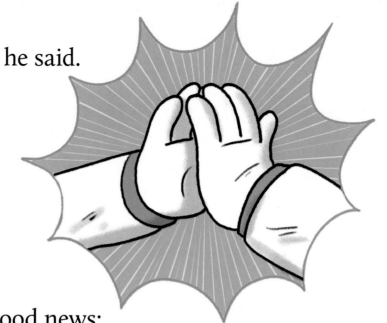

Lingo called Sue with the good news:

Udało się = We did it
przybij piątkę = give me a high five

The view was incredible.

Rex pointed out all the things to see.

"Słońce."

"Ziemia."

ziemia = the earth; **słońce** = the sun

"Księżyc."

"Gwiazdy."

"Robotyczne ramię."

But Lingo spotted something else ...!

Gwiazdy = the stars; księżyc = the moon
robotyczne ramię = the robotic arm

"Mój pluszak!" cried Rex.

Rex's teddy must have floated out of the airlock.

"Użyj robotycznego ramienia," he said.

Lingo was going to use the robotic arm.

mój pluszak = my teddy
użyj robotycznego ramienia = use the robotic arm

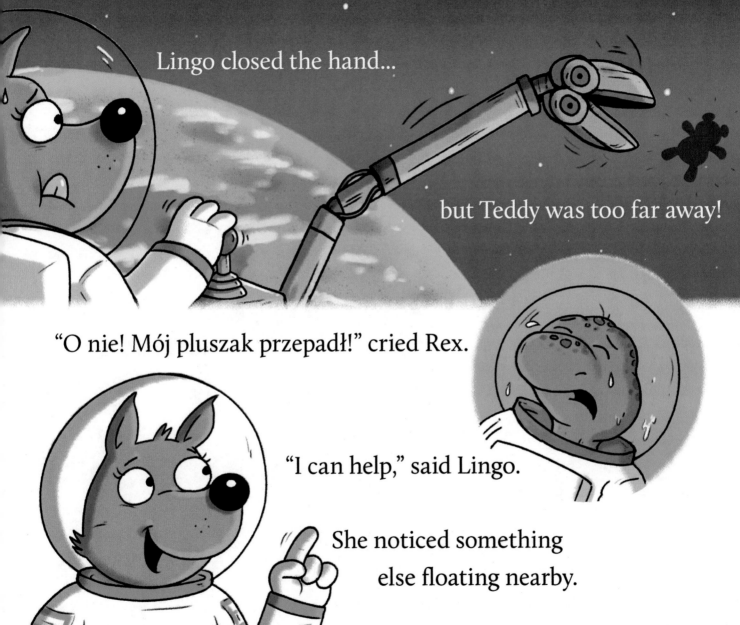

Rex called out the directions: "Góra. Dół.
Prawie. Łap!"

Lingo closed the hand...

but Teddy was too far away!

"O nie! Mój pluszak przepadł!" cried Rex.

"I can help," said Lingo.

She noticed something
else floating nearby.

góra = up; **dół** = down; **prawie** = almost; **łap** = grab it;
O nie = oh no; **Mój pluszak przepadł** = my teddybear is lost

Her fishing rod!

"Trzymaj kciuki," said Rex.

trzymaj kciuki = fingers crossed

Lingo swung the hook

and caught Teddy's bow tie!

"Mój przyjaciel," cheered Rex.
"Uczcijmy to."

mój przyjaciel = my dear friend; **uczcijmy to** = let's celebrate

Rex pressed a button and funky music boomed out.

Time to bust some zero gravity dance moves.

"Ja tańczę, ty tańczysz, miś tańczy, my tańczymy," laughed Rex.

ja tańczę = I dance; **ty tańczysz** = you dance
miś tańczy = teddy dances; **my tańczymy** = we dance

"Uśmiechnij się!" said Rex, and took a photo.

Uśmiechnij się = Say cheese

"Chce ci się pić?" asked Rex. He squeezed big blobs of water over to Lingo. "To jest woda," he said. "Jesteś głodny?" asked Rex.

chce ci się pić? = are you thirsty?
To jest woda = this is water; **jesteś głodny?** = are you hungry?

'Głodny' must mean 'hungry' thought Lingo. "Yes," she replied. "Ja też," Rex agreed.

It was time for space ice cream: "Lody!" he said.

ja też = me too; **lody** = ice cream

Lingo and Rex snuggled into bed.
What an incredible day.

"Uwielbiam kosmos," said Rex.
"Yes," agreed Lingo. "Ja też."
"Śpij dobrze, Lingo" said Rex.

uwielbiam kosmos = I love space

Lingo didn't have time to wonder what 'Śpij dobrze' meant, she was already fast asleep.

Śpij dobrze = sleep well

Learning to love languages

An additional language opens a child's mind, broadens their horizons and enriches their emotional life. Research has shown that the time between a child's birth and their sixth or seventh birthday is a "golden period" when they are most receptive to new languages. This is because they have an in-built ability to distinguish the sounds they hear and make sense of them. The Story-powered Language Learning Method taps into these natural abilities.

How the story-powered language learning method works

We create an emotionally engaging and funny story for children and adults to enjoy together, just like any other picture book. Studies show that social interaction, like enjoying a book together, is critical in language learning.

Through the story, we introduce a relatable character who speaks only in the new language. This helps build empathy and a positive attitude towards people who speak different languages. These are both important aspects in laying the foundations for lasting language acquisition in a child's life.

As the story progresses, the child naturally works with the characters to discover the meanings of a wide range of fun new words. Strategic use of humour ensures that this subconscious learning is rewarded with laughter; the child feels good and the first seeds of a lifelong love of languages are sown.

For more information and free learning resources visit www.neuwestendpress.com

You can learn more words and phrases with these hilarious, heartwarming stories from **NEU WESTEND — PRESS —**

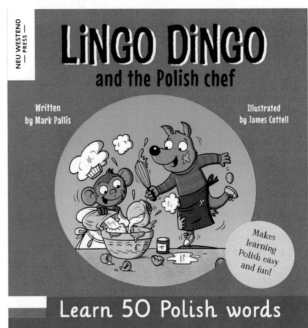

@MARK_PALLIS on twitter
www.markpallis.com

To download your FREE certifcate, and more cool stuff, visit
www.neuwestendpress.com

@jamescottell on INSTAGRAM
www.jamescottellstudios.co.uk

> "I want people to be so busy laughing, they don't realise they're learning!"
> Mark Pallis

Crab and Whale is the bestselling story of how a little Crab helps a big Whale. It's carefully designed to help even the most energetic children find a moment of calm and focus. It also includes a special mindful breathing exercise and affirmation for children.

Featured as one of Mindful.org's
'Seven Mindful Children's books'

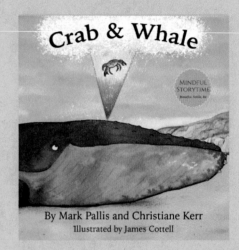

Do you call them hugs or cuddles?

In this funny, heartwarming story, you will laugh out loud as two loveable gibbons try to figure out if a hug is better than a cuddle and, in the process, learn how to get along.

A perfect story for anyone who loves a hug (or a cuddle!)

www.markpallis.com